CHRISTIAN SUPERNATURALISM

Loraine Boettner

GLH Publishing
LOUISVILLE, KY

Originally published in 1937 as a series of articles.
Copyright unrenewed, Public Domain

GLH Publishing Reprint, 2020

ISBN:
 Paperback 978-1-64863-001-9
 Epub 978-1-64863-002-6

*Sign up for updates from GLH Publishing
using the link below and receive a free ebook.*
http://eepurl.com/gj9V19

CONTENTS

1. The Place of the Supernatural in Religion 1
2. Assurance that a Revelation is Genuine 11
3. Extraordinary Providences 24
4. The Alleged Roman Catholic Miracles 32
5. Cures Wrought by the Faith-Healers 39

1. The Place of the Supernatural in Religion

Every thinking person sooner or later reaches the position where he must make some decision concerning the relationship which exists between the natural world in which he lives and the supernatural world which lies above and beyond him. Where do the natural and the supernatural meet, and how are they related to each other? As far back as we can go in human history we find that man has been vitally interested in the origin and purpose of the world and of humanity. Where shall he find the key to the mystery of being? What is the final truth and explanation of all this marvelous system? Man's intellect as well as his moral and religious nature drives him on until he reaches some settled conclusion regarding these matters.

Today, even in religious circles, there seems to be a strong drift away from a frank recognition of the supernatural as a factor in our daily lives. A subtle pantheistic philosophy is abroad, which tends to deny that there is any distinction between the natural and the supernatural. Even the phenomena of life and mind are explained away on materialistic principles. The mainstay of this movement is, of course, the theory of "evolution," according to which we are told that all development, including that of plants, animals, and even man, has been due to an urge inherent in matter as such, by which higher forms are developed from lower. Specifically we may define evolution as *a continuous, progressive change, according to certain laws, and by means of resident forces.* This movement is anti-supernaturalistic to the core, and in many cases has developed into an atheistic naturalism which will know nothing beyond what is given through the five senses.

Since the thinking of the world is to such a great extent actuated by this naturalistic philosophy it is impossible but that Christian thinking should also be influenced in that direction. We find many of the supposedly Christian teachers and writers ruling out as much of the supernatural as they dare; and in some circles the question seems to be not how much of the supernatural was accepted by Christ and the Apostles, but, how little of the supernatural can we have and still call ourselves Christians?

Consequently, the fundamental conflict in which Christianity is engaged today in the intellectual sphere is a conflict between the *Supernaturalism* of the Bible and the *Naturalism* of other systems. Beneath all the attacks lies an undercurrent of Naturalism, sometimes openly advocated, but more often cleverly concealed, depending on whether the person making the attack is outside of or within the ranks of professing Christians.

In regard to the present conflict in the Church those who accept the supernatural are commonly known as "Evangelicals" or "Conservatives," while those who reject the supernatural are known as "Modernists" or "Liberals." The terminology, however, would have been much more accurate had the terms "Supernaturalists" and "Anti-Super-naturalists" been used to designate the two groups, for *Modernism or Liberalism is essentially a denial of the supernatural* more or less consistently carried out. The term "Modernist" is especially misleading since it implies that the formative principle of that system is modern, while the fact of the matter is that the anti-supernaturalistic principle has been held by some groups in every age of Church history.

The more thoroughgoing Modernists start out with the assumption that the supernatural is impossible. Consequently they refuse to recognize anything in nature, life or history outside the lines of natural development, all evidence to the contrary being ruled out of court without examination. The less consistent Modernists retain elements of the supernatural, although there is little agreement among them as to which parts are to be rejected and which are to be kept. Since the system is essentially one of denial, Modernists find it practically impossible to formulate their beliefs in creedal statements. Between such a view of the world and Christianity, it is perfectly correct to say there can be no agreement. Possibly the Modernists may claim that theirs is an improved and purified form of Christianity, but certainly no one can claim that it is the Christianity of Christ and His Apostles.

Modernism, then, offers us a "non-miraculous" Christianity. We are prepared to say, however, that a "non-miraculous" Christianity is simply a contradiction of terms. In order to make our position clear we may define a miracle as *an event in the external world, wrought by the immediate power of God, and designed to accredit a message or a messenger*. Dozens of miracles in this sense are recorded in Scripture. They distinctly were not merely results caused by the application of supposedly "higher laws" which are unknown to us, as some would have us believe. Most of them were works of mercy and healing, although on rare occasions they were used for punishment. We accept them not merely on the report of a credulous and unscientific people, but on the clear testimony of Scripture which we believe to be the Word of God Himself. That the doctrine of miracles is firmly grounded in Scripture is admitted even by those who deny the truth of the doctrine.

Miracle, in the sense of a direct entrance of God in word and deed into human history for gracious ends, is of the very essence of Christianity. The entire New Testament is based on the conception of Jesus as a supernatural Person. Modernism, however, denies not only His miracles, but His deity, His incarnation, His vicarious suffering and death, His resurrection and His claim to be the final Judge of all men. Modernism also rejects an external authority, represents sin as a necessity of development, and nullifies the true conception of sin by starting man off at a state but little removed from that of the brute, while Christianity asserts most emphatically that man has an external Ruler and Judge, and that sin is not something which belongs to the Divine idea of the human race but rather something which entered the race when man deliberately turned aside from his allegiance to his Creator and from the path of his normal development. In other words Christianity involves the idea of a Fall as the presupposition of its doctrine of Redemption, whereas Modernism asserts that the so-called Fall was in a reality a *rise*, and in effect denies the need of any redemption in the Scriptural sense. When anti-supernaturalistic Modernism attacks the Christian doctrine of redemption, and seeks to evaporate it away with a set of platitudes about the guiding hand of God in history, it has assaulted Christianity in the very citadel of its life. With Dr. Warfield we assert that "Supernaturalism is the very breath of Christianity's nostrils, and an anti-supernaturalistic atmosphere is to it the deadliest miasma." Christianity, by its very nature, is committed unreservedly to a belief in the supernatural; and where it has given up that belief it may still exist as a philosophical system, but it has forfeited every right to be called historic Christianity. As Christian men we must assert with all possible emphasis the purity and absoluteness of the supernatural in redemption and revelation.

BELIEF IN THEISM AND BELIEF IN THE MIRACULOUS

We wish to call special attention to the fact that if we are theists as opposed to atheists, if we believe in a personal, self-existent God who created and who rules the heavens and the earth, we have admitted belief in the great basic principle of the supernatural, which in turn should make belief in miracles, visions, inspiration and revelation a very easy matter. Once the existence of God is admitted the possibility of the supernatural cannot be denied, for God is then the great *super* natural Fact. The atheist cannot believe in miracles, for he has no God to work miracles. Neither can the pantheist nor the deist believe in miracles, for the former identifies God with nature while the latter has separated God and the universe so far that they can never be brought together again. But if God exists as the theist believes, if He created and rules the heavens and the earth, no rational person can deny that He has both the power and the knowledge to intervene in the universe which He has made. As Dr. Floyd E. Hamilton has said, "Unless the created is above the Creator, unless the designed thing is greater than the Designer, unless the law is above the Law-Maker, there is no escaping the conclusion that God can, if He wishes, intervene in the universe to carry out His Divine purposes." And as Dr. James Orr has told us, "Many speak glibly of the denial of the supernatural, who never realize how much of the supernatural they have already admitted in affirming the existence of a personal, wise, holy, and beneficent Author of the universe. They may deny supernatural actions in the sense of miracles, but they have affirmed supernatural Being on a scale and in a degree which casts supernatural action quite into the shade. If God is a reality, the whole universe rests on a supernatural basis. A supernatural presence pervades it; a supernatural power sustains it; a supernatural will operates in its forces; a supernatural wisdom appoints its ends. The whole visible order of things rests on another,—an unseen, spiritual, supernatural order,—and is the symbol, the manifestation, the revelation of it."

For the theist the occurrence of any particular miracle becomes simply a matter of evidence. If the existence of natural law in the world proves that miracles are impossible, they also prove that God cannot exercise a providential control over the world and that prayer cannot be answered. Furthermore, the logical corollary to this is that if opposition to the supernatural is consistently carried out, it cannot stop with the denial of miracles, but must carry the person straight over into agnosticism or atheism. It is the height of inconsistency for the Modernist to admit the existence of God, and yet to deny the miracles recorded in Scripture on the ground that they are opposed to natural law. A little reflection should convince any one that the whole theistic conception of the universe is at stake in the denial of miracles.

The Person of Christ and the Doctrine of Miracles

The basic assumption of the Christian system is that Jesus Christ was and is a truly Divine Person, the second Person of the trinity, who at a certain period in history came to earth and took upon Himself our humanity, in whom dwells the fulness of the Godhead bodily, and who, therefore, is to be honored, worshipped and trusted even as God is. If Christ was, as the Scriptures teach, a Divine Person, the miracles recorded of Him are only what we would normally expect of such a Person, so that, as Dr. Warfield has so beautifully expressed it, "When our Lord came down to earth He drew heaven with Him. The signs which accompanied His ministry were but the trailing clouds of glory which He brought from heaven which is His home."

The miracles are not mere appendages to the story but are so bound up with the life and teachings of Christ, so woven into the very warp and woof of New Testament Christianity, that their removal would not only destroy the credibility of the Gospels, but would leave Christ Himself a personage as mythical as Hercules. They were the normal expression of the powers resident in His nature,—sparks, as it were, which revealed the mighty fires within. They stand or fall with the supernatural Person of Christ and with the nature of the work He is said to have accomplished by His suffering and death. If He was a truly supernatural person who vicariously suffered and died in behalf of others, and who arose in a resurrection, they are to be accepted as genuine. If on the other hand we take the view of present-day Modernism that Jesus was only an ideal man, the fairest flower of humanity but nothing more, they must be rejected as incredible. The difference between a Divine Christ with genuine miracles working out a supernatural redemption, and a merely human Christ who is a remarkable teacher and example but who has no power to work miracles, is the difference between two totally diverse religions. It is high time that we do some clear thinking and that we accept the Christ of the New Testament as our Lord and Saviour, or that we reject Him and His miracles as does present-day Modernism.

Ways in Which God Reveals Himself

If, as the Scriptures tell us, God is a personal Being and has created man in His own image, it seems most reasonable to believe that He would have communion and fellowship with the being which He had created. That He should isolate Himself from man would seem most unnatural. Since man was created a free agent and was given a choice between good and evil, it would certainly have seemed strange for God not to have revealed to him the purpose He had in placing him here. Furthermore, if it is true that every man has an immortal soul which is to spend eternity either in heaven or in hell it would seem most unnatural and unreasonable for God to have left him in ignorance of those momentous facts. If man's eternal weal or woe is determined by the course he charts for himself during a short lifetime upon this earth with no further chance after death to correct his mistakes, he must know something of the issues which are being decided. And most of all, if after man has fallen into sin God plans to redeem him and to bring him to salvation through a crucified and risen Lord—through a redemption which was purchased only at an infinite cost to Himself—then a direct intervention of the heavenly Father in behalf of His bewildered and helpless children is in the highest degree probable.

Since it is, therefore, not only possible but highly probable that God would have revealed Himself to man, we next ask, In what ways could that revelation have been given? We find that there are at least five ways in which such a revelation might have been given, and in which, in fact, the Scriptures declare that God has revealed Himself. In the first place He might have revealed Himself directly, appearing in what is called a *theophany*, in which He would have been personally visible and would have talked with man face to face. This is probably the way God spoke to Adam in the Garden of Eden, and would probably have been the most natural and ordinary way for Him to have spoken in later times had it not been for the fact of sin. But when man corrupted himself he destroyed that intimate companionship and erected a barrier between himself and God which has been broken through only on very rare occasions. Since the Fall man has been afraid of God, He has instinctively felt that he could not look upon the face of God and live. Consequently we would not expect that many revelations would have been given in that manner.

In the second place revelations might have been given through dreams, in which case the revelation would have been placed in the mind while man was in an unconscious state; or through visions, in which case the revelation was external to man and was seen or heard through the ordinary faculties. This method, the Scriptures tell us, was very commonly used.

In the third place God might have supernaturally enlightened the minds of chosen men, causing them to perceive clearly the spiritual truths which they in turn were to speak to the people. This method was used in practically every period of the Old Testament era, as well as at the beginnning of the Christian era. Time and again the prophets repeated the words, "Thus saith the Lord," and then proceeded to give forth the messages which God had given to them.

In the fourth place, it was possible for God to so influence certain prophets and apostles that they would write the messages which He wished given to the people. This influence was exerted through the superintending power of the Holy Spirit, and is known as "inspiration." On some occasions this practically amounted to dictation. On other occasions the writers made full use of their native talents as they deliberated, recollected and poured out their hearts to God, the Holy Spirit exercising only a general influence which led them to write what was needful and to keep their writings from error.

The fifth and most important way God revealed Himself was through His only begotten Son, who was both God and man, and who while existing in human form came into very intimate personal relations with His fellow men. This was, beyond all others, the clearest, fullest and most advanced revelation that man has received.

2. Assurance that a Revelation is Genuine

Granted that any person has received a revelation, it would also follow that he should be able to give some proof to his fellow men that he does possess such a revelation. Otherwise he would not be believed. In our human relations whenever some one comes to us claiming to represent another person or institution we demand that he present his credentials. We have a right to demand credentials, and they must be of such a nature that they cannot be duplicated by any other person. Likewise, the prophet who comes with a message from God must be able to show his credentials, and they must be of such a nature that they cannot be duplicated. They must accredit him as a true representative of the court of heaven. Hence it seems very reasonable to expect that in the course of God's dealings with the human race certain men would have been accredited as His messengers and would have been given power to do works of a supernatural order.

These unique works of the prophets and apostles bear the same relation to the works of later ministers and missionaries that the Apostolic office bears to the pastoral office. The extraordinary gifts belonged to the extraordinary office. The prophets and apostles not only worked miracles but possessed the gift of inspiration and wrote books which we acknowledge to be the

Lord's word to the people; but this gift is not possessed by present-day ministers. Revelation and miracles go together while the former remained in the Church, the latter remained also; but when the process of revelation had been completed with the work of Christ and the explanation of that work by the apostles, miracles also ceased. A new era of miracles would indicate a new era of revelation. We believe, however, that with the closing of the New Testament Canon revelation was completed and that we are to expect no more such works until the end of the world.

We have said that the chief purpose of a miracle is to accredit a message or a messenger. This is also clearly stated in Scripture by the Apostle John who wrote, "Many other signs therefore did Jesus in the presence of the disciples, which are not written in this book; but these are written, that ye may believe that Jesus is the Christ, the Son of God; and that believing ye may have life in His name" (John 20:30, 31); and again by the writer of the epistle to the Hebrews, who tells us that the message of salvation which was first "spoken through the Lord, was confirmed unto us by them that heard; God also bearing witness with them, both by signs and wonders, and by manifold powers, and by gifts of the Holy Spirit" (2:3, 4).

Miracles are not to be put on a level with the tricks of a magician or of a wonderworking fakir. Yet it is probably no exaggeration to say that nine-tenths of the opposition to the Christian doctrine of miracles is due to the fact that this distinction is not kept in mind. It is not the bare possibility of miracles which may happen at any time and in the hands of any kind of people, that we contend for, but miracles as an integral part of God's plan of redemption as that plan was made known to a lost and unbelieving race. That, we hold, was a sufficient cause for setting aside the ordinary laws of nature on certain occasions. We readily grant that uninspired men cannot work miracles, and that the age of miracles ceased when the Apostles had given their last message to the world. Consequently we insist that when men discuss the miracles of Scripture they must not beg the question by putting those miracles in an environment foreign to that in which the Scriptures put them. They must not be considered in an abstract manner, but as an integral part of the Christian system of redemption.

MIRACLES AND THE SUBSTANCE OF CHRISTIANITY

It is important to point out that apart from their evidential value certain of the miracles such as the incarnation and resurrection enter into the very substance of Christianity to such a degree that apart from them there is no such thing as Christianity. We know, for instance, that many miracles were wrought which have not been recorded in the Bible, and we readily acknowledge that some of those recorded might have been left unrecorded without seriously impairing the Christian system; but such miracles as the incarnation and resurrection are so vital to the system that their omission would leave us with a radically different religion. For by the incarnation God was enabled to enter personally into the human race, and as the God-man, Jesus Christ, in His capacity as the federal head and representative of His people He took upon Himself the penalty due to us for sin, suffered and died for us on the cross and thus redeemed us; and also as the God-man, in His capacity as the federal head and representative of His people, subject to all of the trials which befall human nature, He overcame all temptation and perfectly kept the moral law (which our former head and representative, Adam, failed to keep) and thus earned for us eternal life. And by the resurrection He as federal head and representative of His people triumphed over death, came forth from the grave with a glorious body, and calls His people to a life of eternal happiness and joy. Paul spoke only the solemn truth when he declared, "If Christ hath not been raised, then is our preaching vain, your faith also is vain.... If Christ hath not been raised, your faith is vain; ye are yet in your sins"; and again, "If we have only hoped in Christ in this life, we are of all men most pitiable" (1 Cor. 15:14, 17, 19). Hence the miracles of incarnation and resurrection are such vitally important parts of the Christian system that if they are omitted what we have left cannot rightly be called historic Christianity.

THE PURPOSE OF PROPHECY

Another way in which God can accredit a revelation to man is through the foretelling of events, or predictive prophecy. This, in reality, is a miracle in the realm of knowledge, a supernatural unfolding of future events. The principal value of a miracle worked in the physical world is to accredit a revelation immediately to the people to whom it is given, while the principal value of prophecy is to accredit the revelation to people who live years later and who see its fulfillment. The Lord alone is able to declare the end from the beginning, and to make known the things which are yet to come. After the prediction has been fulfilled we look back and realize that only a person with supernatural knowledge could have made the prediction, and consequently we accept the remainder of his message as also true.

2. Assurance that a Revelation is Genuine

By prophecy, in the sense of foretelling events, we mean not mere general statements or shrewd guesses such as a person might make by closely observing present tendencies. In every-day conversation the term is sometimes used in that sense, but not properly so. We mean rather the foretelling of events in such detail that only the hypothesis of supernatural knowledge can adequately account for their fulfillment. Today in America, for instance, the political observers with best intellect and keenest insight are not able to predict with any accuracy what the political fortunes of this country will be during the next four years, much less can they predict what these fortunes will be during the next four hundred years. What person forty years ago could have predicted in detail the two world wars, or the rise of Bolshevism, Fascism, or Nazism? Or who today would dare to prophesy in detail the political conditions of Europe twenty-five years from now? And yet we find that the Old Testament prophets did this time after time. Some of the events which they prophesied were not to be fulfilled until centuries after the prophecies were written, and they were set forth in such detail that they cannot be accounted for by anything less than supernatural revelation. We know, for instance, that the Scriptures of the Old Testament were written centuries before the time of Christ. Consequently when we find prophecies foretelling the very town in which He should be born, the virgin birth, the sojourn in Egypt, numerous things about His manner of life and public ministry, and some fifty prophecies which were fulfilled in detail at the time of His crucifixion and resurrection, we have convincing proof that the Scripture writers had supernatural knowledge and that the messages which they gave really came from God. Dr.

Floyd E. Hamilton, in his admirable book, "The Basis of Christian Faith", quotes authority for the statement that "there are in the Old Testament three hundred and thirty-two distinct predictions which were literally fulfilled in Christ." He goes on to say, "The mathematical probability that these would all be fulfilled would be represented by a fraction having one for the numerator and eighty-four followed by ninety-seven ciphers as the denominator!" Fulfillment of the many Scripture prophecies, with never so much as one case of error, is the strongest possible evidence that the Bible is the word of God.

"I declare the end from the beginning, and from ancient times things that are not yet done," says the Lord (Is. 46:10). Listen to Jehovah's challenge to the idol-gods of Babylon to predict future events: "Produce your cause, saith Jehovah; bring forth your strong reasons, saith the King of Jacob. Let them bring them forth, and declare unto us what shall happen: declare ye the former things what they are, that we may consider them, and know the things that are to come hereafter, that we may know ye are gods" (Is. 41:21–23). The dumb idols of the heathen of course know nothing concerning the future, nor can man of himself predict what is going to happen except through a vague and indefinite system of guesswork. But Jehovah, who made this challenge, has fully demonstrated His power to predict the future. He has done so in His holy word, the Bible. Several other nations and sects possess books of a religious nature which they call "sacred books." Not one of them, however, dares make predictions concerning the future. Had the writers of any of those books dared predict the future they would by that very thing have furnished the strongest evidence of their deceptions. Among all of the world's thousands of books, sacred or otherwise, the Bible is the *only* book which contains predictions, and it is preeminently what no other is or can be, a book of prophecy. The fulfillment of these prophecies has shown it to be a supernatural book, a revelation from God. In view of this fact it is a great misfortune that the professing Church of our day almost completely neglects and ignores the study of prophecy. The result is that the Church has lost one of its most powerful weapons against infidelity, and that the denial of the inspiration of the Bible has become very widespread. Such denial could not flourish if the facts were presented. We may also add that this neglect has given occasion for the rise of perverted sects such as Russellism and extreme dispensationalism, whose strength is found mostly in their appeal to prophecy.

Miracles and the Laws of Nature

Perhaps the chief reason that so many men of our day reject the supernaturalism of the Bible is because of a common and widespread belief that the "laws of nature" render miracles impossible. Everywhere about us we see the uniformity of natural law. That the laws of nature do exist is acknowledged as definitely in the Bible as in science. In general such uniformity is necessary in order that we may plan for the future and have the assurance that industry and thrift will be rewarded. Unless nature was thus steady and reliable the world would not be a place in which we could live and work, but rather a crazy system of chance in which anything might happen at any time. The laws of nature are, in the final analysis, merely God's will as to how the material universe should behave. They were established by the creative power of Him who has given to every creature its nature and has appointed its bounds and limits, who established the earth, and by whose ordinances it is governed (Ps. 119:90, 91). The reason they are so uniform is because God is a rational, omniscient, all-powerful Being, whose plan for the universe was worked out in eternity and is caused to move steadily toward its goal. They reflect His power and wisdom. They also are symbols of His constancy and faithfulness.

We hold that nature is neither self-existent nor self-made, but that it is a manufactured article. As Christians we maintain that God *created* the heavens and the earth, and that the work of creation was in the strictest sense a *super*natural work. Consequently we believe that God is not only immanent in matter but that He is transcendent over matter, and that the great sphere of His life and activity lies above and beyond this world. We hold that it is inconceivable that His dealings with the human race should be confined to the limits of the laws which He has ordained for the regulation of material substance, and we affirm that it is His prerogative to set aside or supersede these laws whenever He sees fit to do so.

And when we come to investigate more carefully the character of these "laws" we soon discover that they are not themselves forces in nature, but are merely general statements of the way in which these forces act so far as we have been able to observe them. They are not powers which rule all nature and force obedience to themselves, but rather mere abstractions which have no concrete existence in the external world. They are not eternal and absolute, but were brought into existence and implanted on nature at the time of the original creation. Furthermore, God is under no compulsion to keep them forever uniform, but may set them aside whenever it better serves His purpose to do so. As Dr. Shedd has well said, we must remember that "the order of the universe is a means, not an end, and like other means must give way when the end can be best promoted without it. It is the mark of a weak mind to make an idol of order and method, to cling to established forms of business when they clog instead of advancing it." Granted that we have a personal God and that He has implanted these laws upon the universe which He has created, there is no reason why He may not alter these laws on occasions if He so desires. It is utterly derogatory to the character of God to assume that He is subject to external laws, especially to the laws of matter. He has not imprisoned Himself within His own material creation.

Spiritual Values Superior to Material Values

As Christians we believe that the redemption of the human race from sin was a sufficient cause for God on occasion to set aside the ordinary laws of nature and to work above or contrary to them. We believe that in the Bible we have evidence which proves that He has intervened and that miracles have occurred. We hold that when the human race, which was the thing of primary value in this whole creation, had fallen into sin and was to be redeemed from sin, the laws of nature were not to be considered such fixed and sacred things that God could not move except within their limits, that the moral and spiritual development of human souls was of more importance in His sight than was the uniformity of nature.

The Scriptures tell us of the disastrous fall of the human race into sin; and since we believe not merely in a God of physical order but primarily in a God of holiness, we regard it as most becoming for Him to intervene. Consequently, the incarnation, the atonement, the resurrection and such other revelations and confirmatory signs as He sees fit to give not only commend themselves to us as satisfying our human needs but as most worthy of a God of moral perfection. In such a situation the presumption against miracles is changed into a presumption in their favor, and we are prepared to find the Scriptures setting forth a redemptive process which is supernatural to the core.

We are not then, considering miracles and the supernatural in the abstract, as random or chance happenings, but in relation to a loving heavenly Father and His plan of redemption for a sinful race. We readily grant that sporadic, inconsequent miracles would prove nothing, and would themselves be hard to prove. If we were to hear a report that a miracle had recently been performed in England or Argentina, we would have very serious doubts about the truth of that report; and further investigation would most likely prove that our doubts were well founded. The bare possibility of a leper having been immediately healed, or of a dead man restored to life, viewed simply from the standpoint of present-day physical science, is not an adequate or correct statement of the issue which has been raised by Christianity. But given a supernatural crisis, a supernatural Teacher and a supernatural revelation, miracles are found to be in order like jewels on the state robes of a king. In fact their absence would be unaccountable. To tear miracles out of the great moral and spiritual framework set forth in the Christian system and to treat them as isolated events is as unreasonable as to attempt to study a comet apart from the general system of astronomical laws and forces to which it belongs. Miracles need give no offense to any persons except those who would place the mechanical order of nature above the moral and spiritual order.

It should be clearly understood that there is no conflict between true religion and true science. Religion and science operate in different spheres, — or perhaps it would be more accurate to say that the spiritual and the physical are the opposite poles of the sphere of truth. The task of science is the observation and classification of facts in the *material* realm. True science confines itself strictly to the realm of material things and expresses no opinion whatever as to the reality of the supernatural, as to whether or not miracles have happened or can happen. It is not science but *philosophy* which passes behind the scenes of our material existence and expresses opinions about the causes which are at work there. Science may, indeed, furnish part of the data which the philosopher uses in constructing his system, but there its authority ceases. The scientist may also be a philosopher, but the two roles must not be confused. We insist that the authority of science must not be claimed for statements which in reality are only philosophical deductions. True science neither confirms nor opposes the Christian view of the world which underlies the doctrine of miracles.

Those who advocate the Christian doctrine of miracles, then, are not champions of chaos in an ordered world. Rather they are zealous for law and order of a higher type, that of the spiritual realm, which they hold has been thrown into chaos by man's choice of evil. They point out that sin, disease, sorrow and death are unnatural and abnormal in an ideal world, and that the great majority of the Scripture miracles had as one of their purposes the restoration of order in those regards. In the highest sense they were not violations but restorations of order. They show that the God of spirits is also the God of nature, that spirit and personality are superior to matter, and that the world is held together not merely by physical or mechanical force but by love and holiness.

The tendency of present-day Modernism, of course, is to merge everything into nature and to admit of no other causes. What the Modernist needs to prove, therefore, is not simply that natural causes operate uniformly, but that every physical effect must have a physical cause. That, however, he is unable to do, and that, we hold further, no one except an atheist has a right to assert. In our own natures we find that mind influences matter,—we will to walk or run, to play a piano or to lift a weight, and the effect of mind on matter is clearly seen. We do not understand how the result is accomplished, but we know that it is very real. And if God has so arranged it that our wills produce these physical effects, certainly there is no reason for denying that His omnipotent will may produce infinitely greater effects.

To the objection that we cannot be sure that any particular event is a miracle since we cannot determine with certainty the boundary between the natural and the supernatural, we reply that there are some classes of events about which no person can really doubt, e.g., the raising of Lazarus from the dead, the cleansing of the leper by a touch of the hand, the multiplying of the loaves and fishes, and Jesus' walking on the waters of the sea of Galilee. We may not know the exact boundaries of the natural, but no one can doubt that these events far transcend those boundaries.

2. Assurance that a Revelation is Genuine

Some people are in the habit of using the word "miracle" in a very loose sense, meaning any unusual event such as a remarkable surgical operation, the working of a new chemical or of a new electrical appliance. These, however, are not real miracles, but events which can be explained by the ordinary laws of nature if we are familiar with them.

3. EXTRAORDINARY PROVIDENCES

There is another class of events recorded in Scripture which may be more accurately referred to not as miracles but as "extraordinary providences." In these cases the Lord simply directs the forces which are already at work in nature so that they serve His purposes. Examples are: most of the plagues which came on the Egyptians, the flight of quails which brought meat to the Israelites in the wilderness, the fall of the walls of Jericho if by an earthquake, the great draught of fishes recorded in the Gospels, the rolling away of the stone from the mouth of the tomb of Jesus on the resurrection morning which Matthew specifically tells us was caused by an earthquake, etc. The importance of these events is not lessened by their being put in a separate class, for while not strictly miraculous they do give clear evidence of Divine intervention. There was nothing miraculous, for instance, in the locust plague considered in itself, for such plagues have continued to visit Egypt even to the present day; but when the plague came at the exact time that Moses as the Lord's spokesman had said that it would come, and departed at the appointed time, or when the quails came in great numbers to the right place and at the very time Moses had promised, or when the walls of Jericho fell at the appointed time, then, these events, taken in connection with the words of the prophet, became as clear evidence of Divine intervention as if they had been pure miracles. They proved the prophet to be the messenger of Him who controls the laws of nature and uses them to serve His purposes.

Throughout the Bible the laws of nature, the course of nations, the varying fortunes of individuals, are ever attributed to God's providential control. All things, both in heaven and earth, from the seraphim down to the tiny atom, are ordered by His never-failing providence. So intimate is His relationship with the whole creation that a careless reader might be led toward pantheistic conclusions. Yet individual personalities and second causes are fully recognized—not as independent of God, but as having their proper place in His plan. "To suppose that anything is too great to be comprehended in His control," says Dr. Charles Hodge, "or anything so minute as to escape His notice; or that the infinitude of particulars can distract His attention, is to forget that God is infinite.... The sun diffuses its light through all space as easily as upon any one point. God is as much present everywhere, and with everything, as though He were only in one place, and had but one object of attention." And again, "He is present in every blade of grass, yet guiding Arcturus in his course, marshalling the stars as a host, calling them by their names; present also in every human soul, giving it understanding, endowing it with gifts, working in it both to will and to do. The human heart is in His hands; and He turneth it even as the rivers of water are turned."

And with this agree the Scriptures, for we read, "Jehovah doeth His will in the whirlwind and in the storm, and the clouds are the dust of His feet," Nahum 1:3. "He maketh His sun to shine on the evil and the good, and sendeth rain on the just and the unjust," Matt. 5:45. The famine in Egypt appeared to men to be only the result of natural causes; yet Joseph could say, "The thing is established of God, and God will shortly bring it to pass." The Lord sent His angel to shut the mouths of the lions so that they should not hurt Daniel, Daniel 6:22. "Behold the nations are as a drop in the bucket, and are accounted as the small dust of the balance; behold, He taketh up the isles as a very little thing," Is. 40:15. "He changeth the times and the seasons; He removeth kings, and setteth up kings," Daniel 2:21. "A man's heart deviseth his way, but the Lord directeth his steps," Prov. 16:9. "It is God who worketh in you both to will and to work, for His good pleasure," Phil. 2:13.

MIRACLES ARE NOT WORKED TODAY

We should say further that we believe the age of miracles is past. They do not simply appear at random on the pages of Scripture, but are inseparably connected with periods in which God is revealing His will and plan to His people. When any are reported today we are inclined to reject them outright. We believe that the revelation of the plan of salvation for the world was a fully sufficient cause for miracles in order that that infinitely important revelation might be adequately accredited. Since New Testament times, however, it has been God's purpose not to introduce new and unneeded revelations but to spread this one completed revelation, which is the Christian Gospel, throughout the world, and to bring mankind to a saving knowledge of this truth. Having received the Christian Gospel, the world is not in need of newer and fuller revelations, but needs only to be brought to a saving knowledge of the truth which has already been given. The abundant display of miracles during the public ministry of Jesus and in the Apostolic Church is a mark of the richness and fulness of revelation in that age; and when that period closed, miracle working passed away as a matter of course.

This is also the view of miracles taught by John Calvin. When at the time of the Reformation the Roman Catholics pointed to their alleged miracles and demanded that the Protestants produce works of a similar kind, Calvin replied that the Protestants set forth no new Gospel, but retained the very same truths which had been confirmed by all the miracles of Christ and the Apostles. It is important to keep in mind that the Scriptures teach that the completed revelation of God is given in Christ, and that in the dispensation of the Holy Spirit that one completed revelation is to be diffused to all mankind. If we keep clearly in mind the truly Biblical purpose for which miracles were given—to accredit a new and divinely given message—we shall find that we have a guiding principle which makes it easy to distinguish between genuine and spurious miracles in Church history.

Many people seem inclined to think that miracles were constantly being performed by the prophets. As a matter of fact they were rare occurrences. As Dr. John D. Davis, in *A Dictionary of the Bible*, says, "The miracles of the Bible are confined almost exclusively to four periods, separated from each other by centuries: (1) The time of the redemption of God's people from Egypt and their establishment in Canaan under Moses and Joshua. (2) The life and death struggle of the true religion with heathenism under Elijah and Elisha. (3) The exile, when Jehovah afforded proof of His power and supremacy over the gods of the heathen, although His people were in captivity (Daniel and his companions). (4) The introduction of Christianity, when miracles attested the person of Christ and His doctrine. Outside of these periods miracles are rare indeed (Gen. 5:24). They were almost totally unknown during the many centuries from the creation to the exodus."

And while God does not use miracles in speaking to us who live in the twentieth century, He does speak to us as clearly, even much more clearly, than He ever spoke to people in olden times. We have His completed revelation given to us in a miracle Book, the Bible. This Book is available for all people at a cheap price, whereas most of the former revelations were given to comparatively small groups, most of whom could neither read nor write. The fact of the matter is that miracles, dreams and visions are elementary aids to faith and belong to the kindergarden stage of revelation. They are like the Law, which, Paul tells us, was the instrument of an earlier age and served as "a schoolmaster to bring us to Christ." God speaks to us through the developments of Church History which we have seen take place during the past nineteen centuries, in which we have witnessed the transformation of individuals and of whole nations through the power of the Gospel, a marvelously rich proof of His guidance of His people. He speaks to us through fulfilled prophecy, which is far more abundant for us than it has ever been for any preceding generation. He also speaks to us through the general intellectual enlightenment which characterizes our age, and through the discoveries which have been made in such sciences as Biology, Chemistry, Physics, Astronomy, etc. There is truth in Thomas Fuller's statement that "Miracles are the swaddling-clothes of the infant Church," and in John Foster's comment that "Miracles are the great bell of the universe, which draws men to God's sermon." It is a greater honor which God bestows on us in that He does not speak to us through those elementary means, but that He appeals to our reason and intellect. Those persons do not display much wisdom who insist that He should still speak to us as in primitive times. For Him to do so would be to address us not as men and women but as children.

Lying Wonders

We are not to receive credulously every sign or wonder which is put forth as a miracle, but must test their genuineness, first, by making sure that they reveal something of the character of God and teach truth concerning Him; and secondly, they must be in harmony with the established truths of religion. Some events are reported today, apparently on good authority, which we can ascribe to no other cause than that they are worked by forces of evil.

Not only do the Scriptures teach that the holy angels have access to this world, that they are "ministering spirits sent forth to do service for the sake of them that shall inherit salvation," and that they guard and keep the Lord's people (Heb. 1:14; Ps. 91:11, 12; Matt. 2:13, 19; 28:2–7; Luke 1:11, 26; 2:10–15; 22:43; Acts 1:10; 5:19; 12:7–10; Gen. 19:1–16). They also teach that the Devil and other fallen spirits or demons have access to this world and that they tempt and corrupt human beings so far as they are able (Gen. 3:1–15; Job 1:6–2:7; Matt. 8:28–32; 10:8; 12:22; Mark 1:23, 24; 7:25–30; Luke 8:12; Acts 10:38; 16:16–18). Although invisible to our eyes, good and bad spirits are constantly about us.

Sometimes the evil spirits work wonders in the realm of nature or in revealing the future. Paul tells us that the coming of the man of sin will be "according to the working of Satan with all power and signs and lying wonders," 2 Thess. 2:9. Our Lord said, "There shall arise false Christs, and false prophets, and shall show great signs and wonders; so as to lead astray, if possible, even the elect," Matt. 24:24; and in the book of Revelation John refers to the "spirits of demons, working signs" (16:14). The Egyptian magicians produced snakes from their rods (Ex. 7:11, 12). They also turned water into blood and produced frogs (Ex. 7:22; 8:7), but could not bring forth lice (Ex. 8:18, 19).

False prophets and sorcerers who attempted to mislead the people of God with their delusions were to be put to death (Deut. 13:1–5; Ex. 22:18), and strict commands were given against consulting those who practiced fortune telling or those who had familiar spirits (Lev. 20:6; Deut. 18:10, 11; 2 Kings 21:6; 2 Chr. 33:6, Is. 8:19). To encourage such things was *sin*, because it led the people away from the true God. Those who consulted them did so in direct violation of God's command, and almost invariably turned out bad, e.g., Saul (1 Sam. 28:8–19); Ahaziah (2 Kings 1:14); Manasseh (2 Kings 21:1–15). The sorcerer Simon was misleading the people and was severely condemned by Peter, Acts 8:9–24). Another sorcerer, Elymas, was condemned by Paul, Acts 13:8–12. The works of such persons were not simply pronounced frauds, although there was doubtless much fraud connected with them; they were pronounced works of the Devil or of evil spirits, and the people were told to have nothing to do with them. Every age has produced its crop of fortune tellers, mind readers, mesmerists and spiritualistic mediums, dangers from which we should flee as from an East India cobra.

These signs, whether wrought in heathen lands or by modern sorcerers, are almost invariably mere

3. Extraordinary Providences

wonders, exhibitions of strange powers, wanton violations of the natural order. By contrast the miracles of Scripture are preeminently works of mercy and healing, the whole bearing of which implies the restoration and confirmation, not the violation, of natural or spiritual law. Some of the people engaged in those works have been frank enough to say that their works were wrought through the power of the Devil. We do not acknowledge such signs or wonders as true miracles, for (1) they are not performed by the power of God, (2) their moral character is bad, and (3) they are not designed to prove that the person who works them is the Lord's prophet.

4. THE ALLEGED ROMAN CATHOLIC MIRACLES

In contrast with the doctrine of the Protestant churches that miracles were given to attest revelation and that when revelation ceased miracles also ceased, the Roman Catholic Church claims that the spread of the Church is also a primary cause for miracles and that in every age God has been pleased to work a multitude of miracles for that purpose. Consequently it points to a body of miracles wrought in these later times as large and imposing as that of any period in Biblical history. Protestants insist, however, that nowhere in Scripture are we told that miracles are wrought for the spread of the Church. Protestants acknowledge that incidentally the spread of the Church, as well as the relief of suffering and distress, were aided by the miracles wrought; but they insist that since New Testament times those objectives are to be accomplished by natural means.

We should hardly think it possible that the superstitions and miracle-tales which flourished so luxuriantly during the Middle Ages could maintain themselves in the light of the twentieth century. We find, however, that the Church of Rome, while existing in the twentieth century, is not a part of it. The fact of the matter is that it is a Medieval church which has survived into the twentieth century, and that isolating its people as much as possible from present day progress and enlightenment, it has continued to live in much the same atmosphere of superstition and credulence as that in which it found itself surrounded a thousand years ago.

We must remember that the Church, in coming into the world, came into a heathen world. After the decrees of Emperor Constantine, first legalizing Christianity and then making it the preferred religion of the empire, Church membership became a popular thing and the people flocked into the Church in great numbers. Some came because they were true Christians, but most of the new adherents came because of the social, political or financial advantages which were to be gained. In many cases they were little more than baptized heathen, and they brought their heathen conceptions into the Church with them little changed except in those things which were plainly contradicted by their Christian confession. In a real sense the Church was in turn conquered by the world which it had conquered. As it made its way ever more deeply into the world, enjoying the favors and privileges which came from governmental approval, it was ever more deeply immersed in a heathen atmosphere—an atmosphere surcharged with belief in supernatural powers and influences. Some of the heathen gods and goddesses were taken over into the Church and worshipped as Christian saints. Those who were superstitious remained superstitious, and there was no end to the wild and fantastic miracles which were supposed to have occurred in connection with the pagan idols and temples. This background made it extremely easy for the people to believe the miracle stories which were told concerning the saints and their relics.

A strange phenomenon in regard to these miracles is that, whereas up until the early part of the fourth century (the time at which the Church was legalized) we find not so much as one single writer among the church fathers who claims to have seen a miracle worked, nor one who names any of his predecessors since the time of the Apostles as having wrought miracles, after we reach the fourth century we have a veritable deluge of miracles. And further, these miracles are not only ascribed to the foremost missionaries and saints of the Church, but are recorded by those missionaries and saints as miracles which they themselves have seen or know of. It is claimed, for instance, that the bones of Stephen were found in Jerusalem in the year 415, that certain parts of them were brought into Northern Africa and Italy, and that everywhere they were taken miracles were worked. At different periods in Church history we find Chrysostom, Gregory the Great, Bernard of Clairvaux, and even the great Augustine declaring in parts of their writings that miracle working had ceased, then in later writings they relate a considerable number of miracles. Augustine, for instance, tells us that he was an eye witness to a miracle in Milan in which sight was restored to a blind man. The interesting thing about the case, however, is that he did not seem to have recognized the miraculous character of the event until several years afterward, and had in the meantime expressed it as his conviction that miracles were no longer being performed.

The church fathers do not claim to have performed miracles themselves, yet they report miracles of every conceivable sort which were supposed to have been worked by saints of earlier times, and then it has usually happened that writers of the next generation or later record miracles which were supposed to have been worked by these men. In regard to Thomas à Becket, of Canterbury (England), we have very full accounts of his life and have many letters which were written by him. In none of these does either he or his contemporaries claim that he could work miracles. The stories of miraculous happenings are confined almost entirely to miracles believed to have been wrought by the power of his dead body or at his tomb. Most of the miracle workers of this period appear to have become so posthumously, the honor being thrust upon them rather than claimed by them, so that there seems to be good ground for the taunt of the unbelieving Gibbon in his *History of the Decline and Fall of the Roman Empire*: "It may seem somewhat remarkable that Bernard of Clairvaux, who records so many miracles of his friend, St. Malachi, never takes any notice of his own, which in their turn, however, are carefully related by his companions and disciples. In the long line of ecclesiastical history, does there exist a single instance of a saint asserting that he himself possessed the gift of miracles?"

Perhaps the greatest shrine of miraculous healings in the entire world is at Lourdes, France, where an apparition of the Virgin Mary is supposed to have been seen in 1858, and where numberless supernatural favors are supposed to have been shown by her to pilgrims who have gone there. Literally hundreds of thousands of persons, we are told, have made that pilgrimage, although most of those have gone because of religious motives rather than because of sickness. The whole atmosphere of the place is said to be surcharged with Mary worship. Lourdes does not register her failures, yet it is known that the proportion is very great. One Roman authority tells us rather apologetically that "Hardly one in a thousand of these come to be cured of any sickness." It is generally understood that only about ten per cent of those seeking cures go away benefited. As with most such shrines, very little is said about the enormous mass of disappointment and despair of those who go away unbenefited.

That some cures have been worked at these shrines can hardly be denied, although to all appearances they are the same in kind and are products of the same forces as those wrought today by Christian Scientists, mesmerists, faith-healers. Some medical schools today, recognizing the power of "suggestion" and of proper mental states, are putting courses in psychiatry into their curriculum. There have been many cases where patients have worried themselves sick because of wrong mental attitudes, or after suffering from neurotic or rheumatic afflictions have failed to note the recovery which the body has made, and when as a result of the right kind of thoughts having been powerfully suggested to their minds suddenly discover themselves in a practically normal condition. Some persons who make pilgrimages to shrines approach them with a mind eminently receptive to suggestion, believing implicitly that a cure will be worked; and then, further aided by the ecstasy produced by solemn religious rites, a most fervent prayer, or an immersion in holy water, have found that faith produced the desired results.

We do not attempt to give a full explanation of these cures; certainly we cannot claim to have complete knowledge of all the forces which may assist in bringing about a cure in such conditions as are usually present at these shrines. There are many other things in our daily lives which we cannot explain, but which nobody supposes to be miraculous. The fact that a thing is inscrutable to us is no sufficient reason for allowing ourselves to be stampeded into acknowledging it as miraculous. There may be, and doubtless are, forces at

4. THE ALLEGED ROMAN CATHOLIC MIRACLES

work in nature which are very improperly understood as yet. These can apply to mind as well as to matter. Their existence is strongly suggested by such things as hypnotism, mind reading, mental telepathy, clairvoyance, etc.

We believe that God alone can work miracles, and that He alone is to receive religious veneration. Consequently when the Christian Scientists claim miracles through the application of a foolish philosophy which denies the reality of sin, disease and pain, or when the Roman Catholics claim miracles as the product of an atmosphere surcharged with the idolatrous worship of the Virgin Mary or with veneration for relics such as dead men's bones, teeth or hair, we deny that true miracles are possible under such conditions. For the infinitely wise and just and holy God whom we worship to perform miracles under such conditions, and not in the congregations of His true saints, would be for Him to contradict His very nature. The fact that these cures are reported not only from Roman Catholic shrines, but from faith-healers in all kinds of cults, even from Mohammedan lands, is proof sufficient that the power which each of them claims is no private possession but is the common property of the whole world, and that it is to be had by men of all religions calling upon their various gods.

Furthermore, most of the reputed cures, when investigated, are found to be false. Hardly one in a hundred of them will stand the test of investigation. There is a great contrast between the simplicity and majesty of the Scripture miracles and the trivial, fantastic, and even repellent nature of so many of the ecclesiastical miracles. Most of this latter type, usually alleged to have been performed at the grave or with the "rotten bones" of some saint—together with alleged pieces of wood from the true cross, a sample of the blood of Saint Januarius which is preserved in the cathedral at Naples and which liquifies once every year, samples of the milk of the Virgin Mary which are claimed by several churches in Italy and France, etc.,—have been barefaced impostures openly justified by the priests on the ground of pious frauds. The fact that they are claimed on behalf of a system which contains so much deceit and evil, and that they are propagated to spread the influence of a church which has been guilty of such inhuman and anti-Christian persecutions down through the centuries is in itself a sufficient reason for rejecting them outright.

5. Cures Wrought by the Faith-Healers

Another class of people who claim to work cures in our day are the faith-healers, Christian Scientists and mind-cure specialists. When a serious attempt is made to investigate these cases most of them, like those of the Roman Catholics, are found to be false. We must acknowledge, however, that some of them have been real. Practically all these latter cases have to do with nervous or mental disorders, rheumatic pains, or afflictions which are little if anything more than imaginary. Occasionally those who have been incapacitated for some time have made greater recovery than they realize, and when in connection with a faith-healer's suggestion they suddenly discover their regained strength they sincerely believe that a miracle has been wrought.

It is common knowledge that many people who think themselves to be seriously sick do by that very means make themselves sick. Every physician can testify that he has been called upon to treat dozens of such cases, and that in treating them his primary task is to get his patients into a different state of mind. In such cases the power of suggestion is much more effective than medicine. The cures of the Christian Scientists are in reality not Mind-cures but mind-cures, wrought by the patient's own change of thought—which, indeed, is the substance of what is asserted scores of times by Mrs. Eddy herself in her book, "Science and Health."

What finally emerges in these cases is a definite boundary which separates that class of cures which can be wrought by mental reactions, and those which cannot. In no cases have broken bones, cancer, spinal meningitis, scarlet fever, etc., been cured, nor have amputated limbs, fingers, or even such things as lost teeth or lost hair been restored. The inability of faith-healers to work cures of this kind is in itself an admission that their cures are not truly supernatural.

Another point to be kept in mind is that comparatively few physicians are good diagnosticians, even though they may have practiced medicine all their lives. Perhaps there is no physician who has not been badly deceived more than once in regard to the nature of the disease he was trying to treat—as the autopsy has shown. This is only natural, since the human body is such a highly complicated organism. Doctors often pronounce a case hopeless, only to be surprised by the patient's recovery. Yet faith-healers never tire of telling how this or that doctor gave up a particular case as hopeless. Few contrasts are more remarkable than the scorn which the average faith-healer has for physicians as healers, and the unbounded confidence which he reposes in them as diagnosticians. If he can say that on the testimony of this or that doctor the case was hopeless, he considers that the end of all argument.

The question before us is not as to whether or not God hears and answers prayer, for we believe firmly that He does—we disagree with the faith-healers, however, in that we believe He answers prayer not by miracles, but in accordance with His general providential control; nor is it a question as to whether or not He heals the sick, for this we also believe. The question is: Does God heal the sick in ways which are truly miraculous, without the use of means? And does that healing take place in such a manner that the use of means is unnecessary, or a mark of a lack of faith, or even of sinful distrust on the part of Christians?

In the first place we would point out that the Scriptures contain no promises of such miraculous healings. The passage in Mark 16:17, 18, which is the chief one relied upon by faith-healers, is now recognized as spurious by practically all scholars.[1] The evidence is that those verses were not in the original, but were added by later copyists. The second most quoted passage is James 5:14, 15: "Is any among you sick? let him call for the elders of the church; and let them pray over him, anointing him with oil in the name of the Lord; and the prayer of faith shall save him that is sick, and the Lord shall raise him up; and if he have committed sins, it shall be forgiven him." As Dr. Warfield has well said, "Here we have nothing but a very earnest exhortation to sick people to turn to the Lord in their extremity, and a very precious promise to those who thus call upon Him, that the Lord will surely hearken to their cry." The thing emphasized is that the sick man should get himself prayed for officially by the elders of the church, which prayer, offered in faith, shall surely be heard. The Lord always answers a sincere prayer, perhaps not in the way we ask, but in the way that is best for us. And in answer to the prayer for the sick, the Lord will raise him up, perhaps physically, but at any rate spiritually, which is more important. In this passage the anointing

---

1 A marginal reference in the American Standard Version reads: "The two oldest Greek manuscripts, and some other authorities, omit from verse 9 to the end. Some other authorities have a different ending to the Gospel."

oil is a secondary thing. Certainly there is nothing here which would exclude the ordinary medical means. Oil was a well-nigh universal remedy in the medical practice of the day, and the passage means that the sick man is to be given his medicine in the name of the Lord. The resources of civilization are ours, and we should avail ourselves of all that science knows, remembering that God is the real physician who takes away sin, sickness and death, and that it is He who gives righteousness, healing and life.

Furthermore, we would point out that we have no more reason to believe that our sicknesses and diseases will be cured without means than we have to believe that if we fail to plow and plant we will nevertheless be given food. As well might we expect to live without eating as to recover from sickness without medicine. Surely faith-feeding is quite as rational as faith-healing. And if diseases are to be cured by faith, then why may not death, which is simply the result of disease or injury, also be eliminated in the same way? If cures are to be had by faith, then each successive cure, each successive victory, should be easier than the last, and the body should become immortal. The Scriptures, however, tell us that "It is appointed unto man once to die" (Heb. 9:27); and not even the most zealous of the faith-healers have been able to overcome that affliction. The Bible knows nothing of the redemption of the body in this life. That, it teaches, is to be accomplished in the next life, at the time of the resurrection. After the most careful study we are convinced that the claims of the faith-healers are false.

To neglect the laws of nature which God has ordained, and to refuse to use means, is to act with presumption and to cast disrespect upon God Himself. We believe that the same laws which we depend upon to bring the harvest of corn and wheat may be equally depended upon to bring the harvest of disease and death which we reap every year. No matter how righteous and holy a person may become, if he violates the laws of nature he must suffer for it. If he walks out of the tenth-story window in defiance of the law of gravity he falls with the same certainty and with the same rate of accelerating velocity as other men. The law of gravity is not suspended because of his good moral character.

While faith-healers denounce the calling of a physician and the use of medicine as "un-Scriptural," "dishonouring to God," and as a certain mark of unbelief, almost every one of them in times especially of their last sickness has done that very thing. This was true of Mrs. Eddy, A. B. Simpson, A. J. Gordon, and others. Mrs. Eddy used eye-glasses instead of overcoming the defects of her eyesight by mind, and is reported to have been considerably annoyed when asked why she did not employ the mind-cure in that regard. She also employed the good offices of a dentist to obtain relief from an aching tooth, and even availed herself of his "painless method" to guard herself against unnecessary suffering. Yet according to her own teaching, the decayed tooth, the jumping nerves and the cruel forceps were only illusions.

A great contrast betweeen the Scripture miracles of healing and the reputed cures of the faith-healers is that so many of the latter are only partial cures, or cures which require a considerable period of time to become effective. But when Jesus healed the result followed immediately and was complete. He did not stop half way. He had only to say, "I will; be thou made clean," and the leper was healed. He opened the eyes of the blind by a touch, and commanded the palsied man to take up his bed and walk. The man's withered hand was restored whole. The blind man saw clearly. The lame man leaped up and walked. Jesus healed all who came to Him; yet it is acknowledged even by faith-healers themselves that the great majority of those who come seeking cures today go away not cured. They usually claim that those who go away uncured do so because of weak faith; yet Jesus healed all who came regardless of whether their faith was weak or strong. Furthermore, if miracles were to be considered common, every-day experiences, normal and not extraordinary, they would attract no particular attention and could not be considered the credentials of the Lord's spokesmen, which was their chief purpose in Biblical times.

Faith-healers are very emphatic in their contention that sickness is always contrary to the will of God, and that only a lack of faith keeps any person from being immediately healed. These claims, however, fail to take into consideration certain Scripture statements which declare that on various occasions God Himself has inflicted the disease or the suffering for wise and beneficent purposes. Miriam was smitten with leprosy in order that she and Aaron might be turned from their sinful course (Nu. 12:10). The Lord struck the illegitimate son of David because of the sin which had been committed (2 Sam. 12:15). The psalmist said, "It is good for me that I have been afflicted; That I may learn thy statutes" (Ps. 119:71.) When Jesus was asked, "Rabbi, who sinned, this man or his parents, that he should be born blind?" He replied, "Neither did this man sin, nor his parents; but that the works of God should be made manifest in him" (John 9:3). The sickness of Lazarus was "for the glory of God, that the Son of God may be glorified thereby" (John 11:4).

Paul was *given* "a thorn in the flesh, a messenger from Satan to buffet him, that he should not be exalted over-much" (2 Cor. 12:7)—a physical handicap which we find was intended for a good purpose, namely, that his eminence and success beyond that of the other disciples should not fill him with pride and arrogance. Though he earnestly "besought the Lord thrice, that it might depart from him," it was not removed. We venture to say that in all the world today there is not a Christian mightier in prayer, more devoted, more Spirit-filled and enlightened than was the Apostle Paul. If God would not remove this affliction, though He was besought so earnestly to do so, certainly the faith-healers should hesitate a bit before censoring the suffering saint of today for a lack of faith which they claim would, if he had it, bring relief to his body. When Paul was told by the Lord that it was better for him to endure this suffering, that the Lord's grace would be sufficient for him, he answered, "Most gladly therefore will I rather glory in my weakness, that the power of Christ may rest upon me" (2 Cor. 12:9). In such cases where God is working out some great and good purpose (which probably is unknown to the person who suffers), no amount of prayer will bring healing. Further, we find Paul leaving Trophimus sick at Miletus (2 Tim. 4:20), and in the realm of practical medicine urging Timothy to "use a little wine for thy stomach's sake, and thine often infirmities" (1 Tim. 5:23).

Even Christ Himself, we are told, "learned obedience by the things which He suffered" (Heb. 5:8); and in bringing many sons into glory it was God's purpose also "to make the Author of their salvation perfect through sufferings" (Heb. 2:10). The writer of the epistle to the Hebrews tells us that "Whom the Lord loveth He chasteneth, and scourgeth every son whom he receiveth" (12:6); and again, "God dealeth with you as with sons; for what son is there whom his father chasteneth not? But if ye are without chastening, whereof all have been made partakers, then are ye bastards, and not sons" (12:7, 8). Instead of sickness being an evidence of God's displeasure, it is oftentimes the mark of His favor. The plain fact of the matter is that there is not so much as one verse in all the Bible which states that God wills that His children should be kept from all suffering and affliction. There are many verses which teach that God chastises His children for their spiritual enlightenment. It often happens that the best saints in the Church, those whose spiritual life is truest and deepest, are called upon to endure the greatest pain, while persons of immoral character often have relatively little suffering.

Health is, of course, the general rule for God's people. In each particular instance we are to pray for healing until it becomes clear that it is not God's will to heal the person; and then we are to pray for grace to bear it, that we may be able to say with Jesus in Gethsemane, "Not my will, but thine, be done." We are to remember further that no affliction can come to the children of God except as it is filtered through the sands of His love, and that it will not continue one moment longer than necessary to serve the wise and good purposes which He has in view. "To them that love God all things work together for good." (Rom. 8:28).

There is a sense in which the Devil is the author of disease and suffering, although he can inflict a penalty only as he receives permission from God. God often temporarily delivers a person over to Satan, that his bodily and mental sufferings may react for his salvation (1 Cor. 5:5). One essential lesson in the book of Job is that the child of God is hedged about by protecting love and infinite power, and that Satan cannot touch him without first obtaining permission. In the New Testament accounts the Devil and the demons were immediately subject to the commands of Jesus.

In conclusion we would say that the chief error of the faith-healers lies in the fact that they confuse redemption itself (which is objective to us and takes place outside of us) with the effects of redemption (which are subjective to us and take place within us). Redemption was worked out for us by Christ, and was completed when He died on the cross. The application of that redemption to our souls and bodies by the Holy Spirit, however, is a long process which is carried forward throughout all of our lives here, and which is not completed until we stand with sanctified souls and glorious resurrection bodies before the throne of God. We are no longer under the curse of sin, but so long as we remain in this world we are subjected to temptations and innumerable times we fall into sin. We are enabled, however, more and more to die unto sin and to live unto righteousness. Likewise, in our physical nature we continue weak, subject to disease and certain to die — death being the last enemy to be conquered. The error of the faith-healers is that they set forth a thoroughly un-Scriptural idea of sickness and pain, and try to appropriate here and now those blessings which are not to be conferred until the process is completed.

Again we say that the question is not whether God hears and answers prayer, for we believe that He does. On numerous occasions the present writer has received unmistakable answers to prayer, in the realm of health and in other affairs. But those answers have come not as immediate miracles, but through means, and in the course of God's providential control of events over periods of time. We have definite promises in Scripture that true prayer will be answered, that what we ask *in Christ's name* will be given (John 14:13, 14; Matt. 7:7, 8; James 5:16). Hence we are not to ask for selfish and vainglorious purposes but rather for such things as we have reason to believe are in accord with His will and for His glory, or for such things as we can qualify with the phrase, "If it be thy will"—remembering that Jesus Himself in His most intense and urgent prayer in the Garden of Gethsemane added, "Not my will, but thine, be done" (Luke 22:42). It often happens that what we ask for and want most would not be good for us, in which cases God answers our prayers in the highest form by giving us not what we ask but what He in His wisdom sees will be best for us.

www.ingramcontent.com/pod-product-compliance
Lightning Source LLC
Chambersburg PA
CBHW010004110526
44587CB00024BA/4016